SCHOLASTIC BOOK GUIDES
Snow Treasure

BY MARIE MCSWIGAN

Scholastic grants teachers permission to photocopy the reproducible pages from this book for classroom use. No other part of this publication may be reproduced in whole or in part, or stored in a retrieval system, or transmitted in any form or by any means, electronic, mechanical, photocopying, recording, or otherwise, without permission of the publisher. For information regarding permission, write to Scholastic Teaching Resources, 524 Broadway, New York, NY 10012-3999.

Written by Gary Davis, for The Learning Source
Cover design by Maria Lilja
Interior design by SOLAS

ISBN 0-439-57238-X
Copyright © 2003, 1990 by Scholastic Inc.
All rights reserved.
Printed in the U.S.A.

1 2 3 4 5 6 7 8 9 10   40   09 08 07 06 05 04 03

NEW YORK • TORONTO • LONDON • AUCKLAND • SYDNEY
MEXICO CITY • NEW DELHI • HONG KONG • BUENOS AIRES

Contents

Overview Chart	4
Management System	4
Story Overview	5
About the Genre	6
About the Author	7
Lesson 1	8
Lesson 2	12
Lesson 3	15
Lesson 4	18
Snow Treasure: A Model for Writing	21
Creative Thinking Reproducible Sheets	25
Student Book Log	29

Overview Chart

Comprehension Skills and Strategies

Drawing Conclusions

Interpreting Character Actions

Interpreting Character Traits

Making Judgments

Predicting Outcomes

Stating Persona Reactions

Literary Concepts

Character

Conflict

Plot

Theme

Management System

Snow Treasure and the accompanying guide may be used in the following manner:

Whole Class: Have the whole class read the book together. The class then responds to the literature through discussions and activities. For this system, each child has a copy of the book.

Small Group: Divide the class into reading groups. The groups can be set up by interest level, topic, or ability. (Remember to have some fluent readers in each group to share their reading with less-fluent readers.) Each group responds to the literature through discussions and activities. For this system, each child in the group has a copy of the book.

Read Aloud: Read the book aloud to the whole class or a small group. This will help less-fluent readers and allow children to hear the language and appreciate the author's technique. For this system, only the person reading aloud has a copy of the book.

Story Overview

Snow Treasure tells how a group of Norwegian children helped to smuggle millions of dollars worth of gold bullion out of Nazi-occupied Norway. Written during the height of World War II, the story shows how even the youngest citizens can aid in the fight against a hated invader. It also shows how these same children can display remarkable bravery.

The story opens in the winter of 1940, as Peter Lundstrom, his sister, and friends play in the snow. Their idyllic life is shattered by news that Nazi Germany will invade Norway. Soon children and adults are all involved in a variety of defense measures. Of crucial importance, however, is the gold bullion housed in the country's banks. According to Peter's father, the local banker, and his Uncle Victor, a widely traveled and much-respected fishing boat captain, the gold must be spirited out of the country before it is seized by the Nazis.

Uncle Victor comes up with a daring plan: the unsuspected *children* will carry the gold bars hidden on their sleds. Taking the gold from its hiding place, they will race with it to another area, closer to the water. From there Victor and his first mate, Rolls, will load it on his boat and eventually get it to America.

When Peter's town of Riswyk is quickly overrun by Nazi troops, the children begin the massive effort to move the gold. They are aided by one of the longest and coldest winters in Norway's history. Also, the clever Dr. Aker concocts a mock epidemic when the overly enthusiastic Nazi Commandant demands that the children quit playing outdoors and return to school.

The group receives a final scare when they discover that a German soldier has learned what they are doing. The soldier, however, proves to be a Polish conscript, Jan Lasek, who is anxious to escape from the Germans and get to America. His disappearance has triggered a huge manhunt, and the Norwegians decide to make a massive effort to get the remaining gold to the sea. During that effort, Peter's group is confronted by a Nazi patrol, and only the boy's bravery and quick thinking prevent the discovery of the hidden bullion. Peter, though, is captured and fears the worst will happen to him. But Jan, working with Uncle Victor, manages to liberate Peter from the German barracks and get him to the ship. As the book ends, Peter, Jan, Uncle Victor and his crew are bound for America with the gold, knowing that their actions have helped Norway.

About the Genre

Adventure/Historical Fiction

Like most adventure stories, from *Treasure Island* to *The Black Stallion*, *Snow Treasure* tells a story of courage and daring in which the characters are capable of meeting virtually impossible challenges, saving others' lives and defeating terrible enemies. This is especially true of *Snow Treasure*, in which a group of Norwegian children manage to slip thousands of pounds of gold bullion past Nazi German invaders in order to prevent the gold from falling into enemy hands. The story, with its message that even the youngest members of a community can help defeat a terrible enemy, is particularly inspiring for young readers.

Some of the most popular adventure stories are ones, like *Snow Treasure*, that tell of seemingly commonplace individuals who are suddenly called upon to rise above themselves and act in a heroic manner. Readers readily identify with "heroes" like this, who exemplify the better things of which people of all ages are capable.

Snow Treasure also qualifies as historical fiction, since there is no real proof that the story happened even though a Norwegian freighter with a multi-million dollar cargo of gold did actually arrive in the United States in 1940. Typical of this genre, the story contains a setting in a time from the past; the use of fictional characters; the use of invented dialogue that reflects the way people spoke at that time; and a plot based on the experiences and events of the period.

Bibliography

Clark, Margaret Goff. *Freedom Crossing*. New York: Scholastic, 1980.

Dodge, Mary Mapes. *Hans Brinker or The Silver Skates*. New York: Scholastic, 1988.

Gray, Elizabeth Janet. *Adam of the Road*. New York: Scholastic, 1987.

Krumgold, Joseph. *. . . and now Miguel*. New York: Scholastic, 1989.

Twain, Mark. *The Adventures of Huckleberry Finn*. New York: Scholastic, 1987.

Twain, Mark. *The Adventures of Tom Sawyer*. New York: Scholastic, 1987.

Wilder, Laura Ingalls. *Farmer Boy*. New York: Scholastic, 1986.

Wilder, Laura Ingalls. *On the Banks of Plum Creek*. New York: Scholastic, 1986.

Yep, Laurence. *Dragonwings*. New York: Scholastic, 1990.

About the Author

Born in 1907, Mary McSwigan spent most of her life in and near Pittsburgh, Pennsylvania, a place that figures as the future home of the characters in *Snow Treasure*. After attending the University of Pittsburgh, McSwigan worked as a newspaper writer and devoted much of her writing career to journalism.

She found time, however, to write books for children, among them *Snow Treasure*, which won the Young Reader's Choice Award in 1945. Other books by Marie McSwigan that readers may enjoy include *Three Is a Crowd*, *Our Town Has a Circus*, and *Bennie Latches On*.

Snow Treasure

Lesson 1

Chapters 1–7 Pages 1–37

Synopsis

During the winter of 1940, while sledding with his sister Lovisa and friends near one of Norway's fiords, 12-year-old Peter Lundstrom is surprised to see his Uncle Victor, the master of a fleet of fishing boats, in Riswyk at this time of year. Upon hearing the news of his brother at supper, Peter's father, a banker, leaves abruptly.

That night, Peter learns what is happening. With Nazi Germany about to invade Norway, the people of Riswyk plan to sneak gold bullion out of town to the Snake (on arm of the Riswyk fiord). There the gold will be put onto Victor Lundstrum's personal ship, the *Cleng Peerson*, and taken to America for safekeeping. Uncle Victor wants the children to sled the gold past Nazi sentries. Peter's father is reluctant to risk the children's safety but agrees that this is the only way to get the much-needed job done. Peter is appointed president of the children's Defense Club, the one whom the other children must obey. Then, at midnight, Peter's father shows him a man-made cave in the woods where the bullion will be waiting for the children.

Early the next day, Uncle Victor brings word that German troops have landed. He explains to Michael, Helga, and Lovisa (the three other team leaders) how to transport the gold. Peter's father leaves them to join the war effort.

Before Reading

Tell students that they will read a book called *Snow Treasure*, a story about how the bravery of a group of children helps in the fight against a terrible enemy. Explain that the book shows what people, even children, can accomplish in a time of need. It also shows how an entire town can work together to accomplish an important goal. In this case, the goal is to keep tons of gold from the hands of an enemy that has invaded the country.

Use the activity that is best suited for your class.

Option 1: Explore the idea of what an *enemy* is by drawing on students' prior knowledge of literature. Talk about the characters who had to deal with real or imaginary enemies. If students have difficulty recalling examples, remind them of such classic tales as *Treasure Island*, in which a boy must deal with an entire band of pirates, or *Johnny Tremain*, in which American patriots are struggling against their British oppressors.

Divide the class into small discussion groups for the purpose of listing the enemies described in books (both fiction and nonfiction) they have read. Have some group members describe these enemies in words while others draw pictures of them. (You may want to suggest that they illustrate the Hessian soldiers who wore bright red uniforms when they fought the Colonists during the Revolutionary War.) When the students have finished, have the groups share what they've done with the rest of the class.

Option 2: For students who are not familiar with other books, help define what an enemy is and have students explore the concept. For example, ask students if they know someone who has fought in a war, having them identify the war, and explain what the causes were, and who the enemy was. Or, if students wish, have them relate instances in which they came up against a real or imaginary enemy. Help students understand that, for both individuals and countries, today's enemy is often tomorrow's friend. When they have finished, have students make a list of words or phrases that people might use to describe how they feel about an enemy. Then ask students to compare lists and discuss why some of these words might appear on so many lists.

Distribute copies of *Snow Treasure* and call students' attention to the illustration on the cover. Identify the first boy as Peter Lundstrom, the other children as Peter's sister Lovisa and their friend, Michael, and the adults as Nazi soldiers who have invaded the children's country, Norway. Explain that this story takes place in 1940, during World War II, in the cold, snowy country of Norway. Ask students what they think the book's title might mean.

> Note: Remind students that the book was published in 1942 during World War II. Explain that a "world" war is fought by the principal nations in the world. World War II was fought during the period 1939–1945 in Europe against Nazi Germany and from 1941–1945 in the Pacific against Japan. Adolf Hitler was the dictator who controlled Germany at that time and invaded countries such as Norway, Britain, and France.

Before beginning the story, tell students that it is a tale of adventure and courage and that the children in it are real heroes. Point out that many people actually believe that this story is true. On June 28, 1940, a Norwegian freighter named *Bomma* reached Baltimore with $9 million in gold. The captain of the ship told the story students will read in *Snow Treasure*. He would not give real names and locations, though, in order to protect the children. Because of this there is no real proof that the story ever really happened, but many people, both in America and Norway, do believe that the events are true.

During Reading

Tell the students to listen as you read Chapter 1 aloud, explaining that in this part of the book, Peter, Lovisa, and their friends are surprised to discover that Peter's uncle is in town so early in the year. Then read pages 1–8 to the class. Ask students to name and describe the four children and their uncle. Ask them to explain why Peter thinks that something strange is happening in Riswyk.

When they have finished, assign pages 9–37 for independent reading. Tell students that on these pages they will learn how the people of Riswyk plan to smuggle the gold out of the country to safety.

Literary Concepts

Discuss setting: Remind students that the *setting* is when and where a book or story takes place. Ask students if they can tell when this story takes place, helping them recognize that the story takes place during the time when Nazi Germany was conquering much of Europe. Then ask students where the story takes place, making sure they understand that the country is Norway and that it is in the northernmost part of Europe. Help students locate Norway on a world map, pointing out its indented coast lined with thousands of islands and its neighbors—Sweden, Finland, and the USSR in the east. Explain that a *fiord* (pronounced fyôrd) is a long, narrow inlet from the sea between steep cliffs or slopes.

Work with the students to complete the following graphic describing the setting of the book:

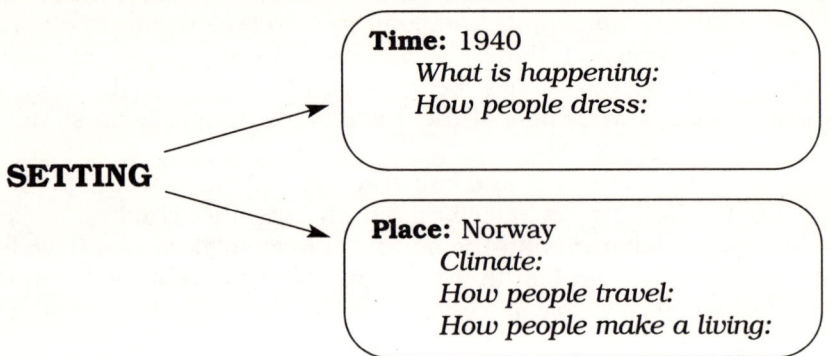

SETTING

Time: 1940
  What is happening:
  How people dress:

Place: Norway
  Climate:
  How people travel:
  How people make a living:

Next, ask students to identify details in these chapters that helped them recognize these facts about the book's setting. Write the items on the chalkboard, creating a list like the following:

   Michael's "typically Scandinavian" appearance

   Sleds

   Victor is in command of the Lundstrom fishing fleet.

   Peter's father is a banker.

   Area is near fiords.

Have students discuss these details, helping them recognize what each is and what it tells them about the book's setting. When they have finished, remind them to look for similar details when they read the next section of the book.

Points to Ponder

1. Why do you think Peter is so drawn to Uncle Victor? *(Interpreting Character Traits)*

2. Do you think Peter will be a good president of the Defense Club? *(Making Judgments)*

3. From what you have read so far, what do you think of the Nazis? *(Stating Personal Reactions)*

4. How would your community react if another country was about to invade it? *(Drawing Conclusions)*

5. Considering the location and climate of the town, do you think the plan for getting the gold out of Riswyk is a good one? Why or why not? *(Making Judgments/ Understanding Setting)*

After Reading

Choose from the following activities:

1. Suppose invaders came to your area. How would you smuggle valuables out of the country? Write a plan that you think would work.

2. Read an encyclopedia article about Norway. Write 10 interesting facts about the country and its people.

3. Imagine that you are Peter Lundstrom and were just told what you would be doing to smuggle gold out of Norway. Write a paragraph describing how you would feel.

4. Pretend that you are the president of the Defense Club. Describe the qualities of a good president.

Sign-up Sheet

Name   *Activity Number*   *Date Started*   *Date Completed*

Snow Treasure

Lesson 2

Chapters 8–14   Pages 38–74

Synopsis

The four team leaders—Peter, Lovisa, Helga, and Michael—pledge never to speak to the German soldiers or to reveal anything about the gold, even if they are caught. Peter then attempts to lead the children to the cave. It is so well camouflaged, however, that he can't find it, and it takes Per Garson, the family servant, to show them the entrance. After Per Garson carefully loads and ties the bullion onto the sleds, he shows the children how to untie it themselves.

Soon the children make their first descent to the beach. The trip is successful, in part because the German soldiers seem to enjoy watching the children on their sleds and make friendly comments that the children do not acknowledge. When the children reach the predetermined spot, they unload the gold and bury it in the snow. They build snowmen over the gold so Uncle Victor and his mate can tell exactly where the gold is buried.

The children then hurry to the Holms' farm, where they spend the night. Every morning thereafter, a group of children descends towards the beach carrying a load of gold. Everything goes well until it starts to rain, threatening to wash away the snow and put an abrupt end to the plan. To everyone's relief, however, the rain turns into a raging blizzard.

Before Reading

Give students some background on World War II, especially on the role Norway played in it.

When Hitler's Nazi armies invaded Poland, in September 1939, England, France, and other countries immediately declared war. Norway, however, tried to remain neutral, not fighting for either side. But on April 9, 1940, Germany invaded, attacking all of Norway's major seaports at once. For two months Norway's armies and people fought as best they could, with help coming from British, French, and even Polish troops. But on June 10, 1940, Norway finally had to surrender, and the Nazis set up a "puppet government," a government made up of Norwegian traitors who followed the Nazis' orders.

The king of Norway. Haakon VII, fled the country and, with key leaders, set up a government-in-exile in London, England. Meanwhile, thousands of Norwegians joined a secret army, called the Resistance, that fought against the Germans. They ambushed Nazi soldiers and blew up German trains, trucks, and military bases. Whenever the Resistance struck, the Nazis, in turn, tortured and killed Norwegians at random, trying to terrify the people into stopping the sabotage. When Allied troops finally defeated the Nazis, in May 1945, the 350,000 German soldiers in Norway surrendered. King Haakon VII returned to his country on June 7, 1945, and peace and Norwegian independence were restored.

Ask students to consider what it must be like to live in a war-torn country. Have them think about this for a while and then discuss how they would feel about enemy troops roaming their community, entering their homes, harassing their friends and neighbors. Have students pretend that they are living in Riswyk on the first day of the German invasion. Ask each child to write a letter to a relative in the United States describing life in Riswyk under the Nazis. To help them write their letters, first have them complete the chart as they imagine life in Riswyk.

Riswyk Before the Invasion	Riswyk During the Invasion

After students have completed the chart, have them begin their letters. Provide assistance as needed and, when students have finished, have them share their work.

During Reading

Assign students Chapters 8–14 to read. Before they read, have students summarize what has occurred in the story through Chapter 7.

Literary Concepts

Discuss plot and conflict: Explain that *plot* is the series of events that takes place in a story. It is the main story line. In most stories, the plot is made up of one or more important problems, or *conflicts*, that must be solved. The problems usually are presented at the beginning of the story. Then, toward the middle, we learn more about them and about the ways in which the characters try to solve the problems. By the end of the story, though, those problems usually are solved in one way or another.

Have students discuss the problems presented in the first 14 chapters of *Snow Treasure*. Have volunteers list some of the problems on the board. Possible answers include: How is the gold going to be taken to the Snake? Will the Norwegians be able to keep what they are doing a secret? Will there be snow for the sleds to ride on? Have each student select one problem and write down how he or she thinks the problem will be solved later on in the book.

Points to Ponder

1. What do you think would have happened had the rain washed away the snow? *(Drawing Conclusions/Understanding Conflict)*

2. Why do you think some of the German soldiers seem so friendly to the children? *(Interpreting Character Actions)*

3. Do you think Peter was brave or foolish for riding his sled so close to the marching soldiers? Explain your answer. *(Stating Personal Reactions)*

4. Do you think Uncle Victor's plan is working well so far? Explain your answer. *(Making Judgments)*

5. Is Peter a good leader for the children? Why or why not? *(Making Judgments)*

After Reading

Choose from the following activities:

1. Read an encyclopedia article about skiing. Where did skis come from? Has skiing ever been used for anything but fun and sport? How did skiing become so popular in this country? Write down what you learn. Illustrate your work with pictures of ski equipment.

2. Draw a picture map of the area described in the book, from the Snake and the fiord up the mountainside to Riswyk. Label your map.

3. Read about sleds and sleighs in an encyclopedia. Where is this mode of transportation important? What is the difference between a sled and a sleigh? What different kinds of sleds and sleighs are there? Give an oral report to the class on your findings.

4. Imagine that you are one of the group leaders of the Riswyk children. Write a letter to your father, who is fighting with the Norwegian army. In your letter tell him what the children have been doing and why you think it is an important thing to do.

Sign-up Sheet

Name   *Activity Number*   *Date Started*   *Date Completed*

_____

_____

_____

_____

_____

_____

_____

_____

_____

_____

_____

_____

_____

_____

Snow Treasure

Lesson 3

Chapters 15–22 Pages 75–117

Synopsis

Peter has an unfortunate encounter with the German Commandant, angering the Nazi officer with his refusal to answer a question. As a result, the Commandant proclaims that all children must return to school, a situation, obviously, which could ruin the town's plan.

With the help of Dr. Aker, the town doctor, Peter's mother concocts an "epidemic" of a strange, new disease to keep the school closed. Dr. Aker then convinces the Nazis that the school must remain closed and that their soldiers should stay away from the town in order to prevent the spread of the unusual disease. As a result, the gold continues to travel down the mountain.

Soon, a Nazi soldier emerges from the woods and skis right by the children. Worried that the entire plan has been exposed, Peter brings the news to Hen Holm who, in turn, sneaks out to Fru Lundstrom's home.

Taking it upon herself to find and warn Victor, Fru Lundstrom takes three small children with her in order to avoid suspicion. Thus informed, Victor decides to speed up the operation. A new crisis is reached a week later, though, when Peter discovers a Nazi soldier watching him build one of the snowmen that marks the buried gold.

Before Reading

Tell students that they have been introduced to most of the important characters in the book. Have students think about the characters and volunteer their names. List the names on the chalkboard.

Explain that you are going to read clues about some of the characters and that the students will be asked to guess the characters' names. Then read each clue below. As the students respond, support any reasonable answers.

- He leads the life of an adventurer. He is one of the most successful fishermen in a land of able-bodied fishermen. *(Uncle Victor Lundstrom)*
- He is the leader of the Defense Club. *(Peter Lundstrom)*
- She is a tomboy who can fight as well as any boy. *(Helga)*
- His bones ache whenever the rain is coming. *(Per Garson)*
- He is a banker who leaves his family to go to war. *(Peter's father)*
- She is the youngest one to lead a team. *(Lovisa Lundstrom)*

Have students continue the activity by finding other good character clues in Chapters 1–14. Have them read the clues aloud and identify the characters.

Then have each student select his or her favorite character and write a paragraph explaining why that character is a favorite. Have students share their choices by reading the paragraphs aloud. Tally the students' choices to see which character is the most popular.

During Reading

Assign the next eight chapters (pages 75–117) for student reading. As they read, encourage students to continue thinking about the characters and how they are alike and different. Direct students to think about traits that all or most of the characters have in common (cooperative, loyal, brave, and so on).

Literary Concepts

Discuss character: Explain that characters in books, just like people in real life, usually have many different traits. Illustrate this by having students name one character from *Snow Treasure*. Then have students suggest single words that describe that character. Write the words on the board and discuss whether each one is accurate. Then have students complete the following chart with other characters and traits from the book:

Character	Traits
Peter	brave

Have students look over their charts to find the traits that were listed most often. You may wish to compile those traits on the chalkboard.

Divide students into cooperative learning groups of three. Assign each group one of the following character traits: cooperative, loyal, brave, reliable. Have students find and record examples from the book in which characters exhibit that particular trait.

Points to Ponder

1. What kind of person does Uncle Victor think Peter is? How can you tell? *(Interpreting Character Traits)*

2. Why do the people of Riswyk refuse to talk to the soldiers? *(Interpreting Character Actions)*

3. Do you think Peter's actions with the Nazi Commandant were wise? Why or why not? *(Making Judgments)*

4. Suppose the Nazi Commandant did not believe Dr. Aker's story about the "epidemic." What do you think might have happened? *(Drawing Conclusions)*

5. What do you think will happen to Peter now that he has been discovered by the Nazi soldier? *(Predicting Outcomes)*

After Reading

Choose from the following activities:

1. Draw the *Cleng Peerson.* Use your drawing to show people how big the ship is and how fast you think it can go.

2. Write about something brave you or someone close to you has done. Describe who did it, what it was, why it had to be done, and what was so special about it.

3. Imagine that you are one of the Riswyk children's team leaders. Write a diary in which you recount the main events of the weeks during which the children have been moving the gold.

4. Interview your grandparents or older neighbors about their experiences during World War II. Prepare a list of questions, such as: "What important historical events did you hear or read about during the war?" "How did you participate in the war effort?" "What sacrifices, if any, did you have to make?" Then, during the interview, write down the answers. Share the information with your class.

Sign-up Sheet

Name *Activity Number* *Date Started* *Date Completed*

Snow Treasure

Lesson 4 — Chapters 23–30 Pages 118–156

Synopsis

The sight of the Nazi soldier shocks Peter. Suddenly, Uncle Victor and Rolls appear and haul the soldier off to the *Cleng*. Peter follows. The soldier tells them that he is not a Nazi but a Pole named Jan Lasek who has been forced into the Nazi army. Victor, however, is not quite convinced and he is certain that the Nazis will immediately start to search for the missing soldier. The *Cleng Peerson* and the entire operation are in danger.

When Lovisa and her group are burying the last of the gold, they see a search party of soldiers nearby. In the course of their encounter, the Nazi Commandant nearly discovers the gold. To stop him Peter throws a hard snowball and hits him on the ear. Peter is caught and locked in a small, dark room in the Nazi barracks. Soon the door opens and there stands Jan Lasek who has come dressed in his Nazi uniform to help Peter escape.

Later, Uncle Victor sets sail for America with Peter and Jan aboard. They and the gold are bound for freedom and safety.

Before Reading

Tell students that they will now be reading the final chapters of the book. Review with students what usually happens at the end of a story. Elicit the following points:

- The problem or problems are often solved in some way.

- We find out what happens to the main characters.

- The message of the story usually becomes clear.

Divide the class into small groups and ask them to think about how *Snow Treasure* might end. Have each group create an ending for the book, making sure that students include a solution to the main conflicts as well as a description of what happens to each main character. Have the groups share their endings, discussing which endings make sense, which are exciting, and which tell us about what happens to the characters.

During Reading

Have students read the final chapters of *Snow Treasure*, Chapters 23–30 (pages 118–156), telling them to think about how each of the characters in the book shows courage.

Literary Concepts

Discuss theme: Remind students that courage, or bravery, is a main theme of *Snow Treasure*. Discuss examples from the book, leading students to see that all of the citizens of Riswyk have behaved very courageously.

Put the following chart on the chalkboard. Then have students complete the chart with at least one example of courage for each character.

Character	Example of Courage
Mrs. Lundstrom	
Victor Lundstrom	
Peter Lundstrom	
Jan Lasek	
Lovisa Lundstrom	

When students have finished the chart, ask them which character was the most courageous. Have them give reasons to support their choices.

Points to Ponder

1. What do you think of the way in which Peter got the Commandant's attention away from the snowman? What else could he have done to save the gold? *(Making Judgments)*

2. What might have happened if Peter had not escaped to America? *(Drawing Conclusions)*

3. What do you think happened back in Riswyk after Peter escaped? *(Drawing Conclusions)*

4. What do you think of Jan Lasek? *(Stating Personal Reactions/Interpreting Character Traits)*

5. What lessons about courage did you learn from this book? *(Understanding Theme/Stating Personal Reactions)*

After Reading

Choose from the following activities:

1. Every ship captain keeps a ship's log that tells what happens on a ship's voyage. Write a ship's log for the *Cleng Peerson* as it makes its way from Norway to America. Describe what might have happened during the voyage.

2. Imagine that you are Peter Lundstrom living in Minnesota. Write a letter to your mother and father back in Riswyk. Tell about your life in the United States and ask about family members and hometown news.

3. Choose three characters from this book that you especially liked or admired. Make drawings of them to show what they looked like.

4. With another student, write a one-act play based on Peter's escape from prison. Then, with you and the other student taking the parts of Peter and Jan, act out the play for the rest of the class.

Sign-up Sheet

Name   *Activity Number*   *Date Started*   *Date Completed*

_____

_____

_____

_____

_____

_____

_____

_____

_____

_____

_____

_____

_____

_____

Snow Treasure

A Model for Writing

The Prewriting Stage

The purpose of prewriting is to use strategies or plans to get ready to write. This stage is critical in helping children get their ideas out in the open through talking, brainstorming, drawing, diagramming, or free-writing.

Many writers turn to people and events in the news for ideas and inspiration. Marie McSwigan, for example, was inspired by the tale told by the Norwegian sea captain who brought the shipment of gold to the United States.

- Encourage students to talk freely about interesting events they have heard about. Ask: "Is there something you heard about—in the news or from what someone told you—that is unusually interesting or important? Is there any factual story that you think other people would like to hear about in more detail?"

- Tell students they will be writing a story based upon real events they have heard about recently. Stories based on real life are often "fictionalized"; that is, make-believe people and events are added so the story will be more interesting. (Point out, for example, that Marie McSwigan probably added descriptions and dialogue to the original story. Discuss with students which characters and details she probably added and where she might have gotten the ideas for them.)

- Form small groups for peer conferencing. Help children direct their thoughts about a particular story—something from a recent magazine, a newspaper story, or something featured on a recent television program.

- Help students create a story summary that gives the basic plot and details of this story. It should include a statement of the story as well as a list of people involved.

- Give the students several days to think about what should be added to their story. They should think about how the story could be made more interesting, what should be added, taken out, or changed in order to make the story's theme come through clearly, and what additional characters might be needed to provide excitement and interest.

- When students have finished, organize an in-class "starter" session. Let students free-write for five to 10 minutes without interference, allowing them to get down on paper their major ideas about the story. Remind them to put down only the most important ideas at this time. Other ideas, as well as spelling, grammar, and handwriting, can be worked on at a later time.

The Drafting Stage

Drafting involves getting your ideas down on paper, focusing on content, and considering the audience and purpose. The emphasis should be on pulling ideas together without concern for spelling or usage.

Model the drafting process by showing students how to decide on what their new "fictionalized" story will be. List two or three changes in your own story that you would like to make (adding events or characters, changing what happens, and so on). Encourage students to work with a partner or small group to write and share their ideas for their stories. Explain that this process will help them develop their thoughts about the story.

To help students start their stories, ask them to think about the following questions:

- Why is the story so memorable?

- When and where does it take place?

- Who are the characters involved?

- Exactly what happens in the story?

- What theme or message does the story have?

- Are there any other events that could be added that would help dramatize the theme of the story?

Then have everyone write, including the teacher. When everyone has finished, ask: "Who would like to share their work today?" You may want to start things off by reading your draft aloud. Structure the time as a whole-class activity or as small-group discussions. Keep all responses positive and constructive.

The Revising Stage

Revising, or taking a second look at what has been written, is at the heart of writing. Children learn strategies and techniques best when these are demonstrated through children's own writings. Some strategies (Calkins, 1986; Zinsser, 1980; Murray, 1983) include:

- Take a short piece and make it longer.

- Experiment with different openings.

- Experiment with different orders—flashbacks, flashforwards, and so on.

- Try telling the story in a different tense.

- Reread the draft, listening to how it sounds.

- Summarize the plot in four or five sequential sentences.

- Try telling the story from a different point of view.

- Talk with someone about your draft, then rewrite it without looking at previous versions.

Show students the following proofreading marks, explaining how they can be shortcuts to making changes during the revising stage:

Mark	Meaning	Example
¶	new paragraph	¶ The children slept. The next morning they woke up to a blizzard.
∧	insert, add this	Peter ∧ Michael would lead the children. (or)
≡	capital letter	The holm farm was dark and quiet.
ℓ	delete, take this out	Peter was frightened and scared.
⌒	transpose, move	Pete harshly glared at the Commandant.
....	stet, let it stay	Helga climbed carefully aboard the sled.

Materials for revising and editing should be kept at the Writing Center: scissors, tape, stapler, correction fluid, marking pens, pencils, and crayons.

Allow the students time to revise their fictionalized news stories.

The Editing Stage

Students should edit once they are satisfied with the content of their pieces. During editing, students reread and correct their writing for word choices, spelling, grammar, usage, and punctuation.

Students may proofread alone or with a partner, either on paper or on a word-processor screen. Some editing techniques (Calkins, 1989) include:

- rereading through the final draft quickly to be sure it says what you want
- looking for key words and asking, "Is this the best word to use here? Does it make the reader 'see' what is happening?"
- checking the spelling and mechanics
- using an editing checklist

Editing materials include: dictionary, thesaurus, spelling guides, grammar and usage charts, editor's blue pencils, and reference books.

Editing makes the most sense to children when it leads to publishing their writings.

The Publishing Stage

Students enjoy and learn from publishing and sharing their writing. Some ways tried by teachers are:

- a class magazine, newsletter, or newspaper
- hand-bound books for the library
- displays of student pieces, drafts, and books
- recordings (on cassettes) that students make of their own writing
- class anthologies
- submitting student writing to outside publications—school or local magazines and newspapers, national magazines devoted to children's literature

Let children help decide the audience(s) with whom they will share their work.

Name: Date:

My Heroes

To many people, the children of Riswyk are heroes. What other real-life heroes do you know of? What did they do? In the space below, make a poster about the hero of your choice. It should show what the person looks like, and tell what he or she did and how people feel about this hero. Be sure to put a title across the top of your poster.

Snow Treasure **Creative Thinking 1**

Name: Date:

Tips for Getting Along

The children of Riswyk got along remarkably well during the time when they moved the gold from the cave. What do you think people need to do in order to get along with one another in an emergency? In the space below make a list of "Do's" and "Don't's" for getting along with other people. Then, on a separate sheet of paper, write a short essay about the need for cooperation during an emergency.

Snow Treasure Creative Thinking 2

Name: Date:

A "Must-See" Movie

Imagine that you are making a movie of *Snow Treasure*. What do you need to tell people to make them want to see this movie? In the space below, make an advertisement for your movie. It should tell the name of the movie and who the actors are. It should have an illustration that will make people interested in the movie, and it should tell them why they should see the movie.

Snow Treasure Creative Thinking 3

Name: Date:

Extra! Extra!

Imagine that you are the publisher of Riswyk's newspaper. What story would you like to put in your paper to tell people about how the gold has been saved from the Nazis? In the space below, write your story. At the top, put a headline that grabs people's attention and tells them what they will be reading about. Then put the story in the two columns below.

Snow Treasure   Creative Thinking 4

Student Book Log

Name: _____ Class: _____

Title	Author	Genre	Subcategory	Date Read	Evaluation 1 (low)—5 (high)	Personal Reaction (Comments)

29

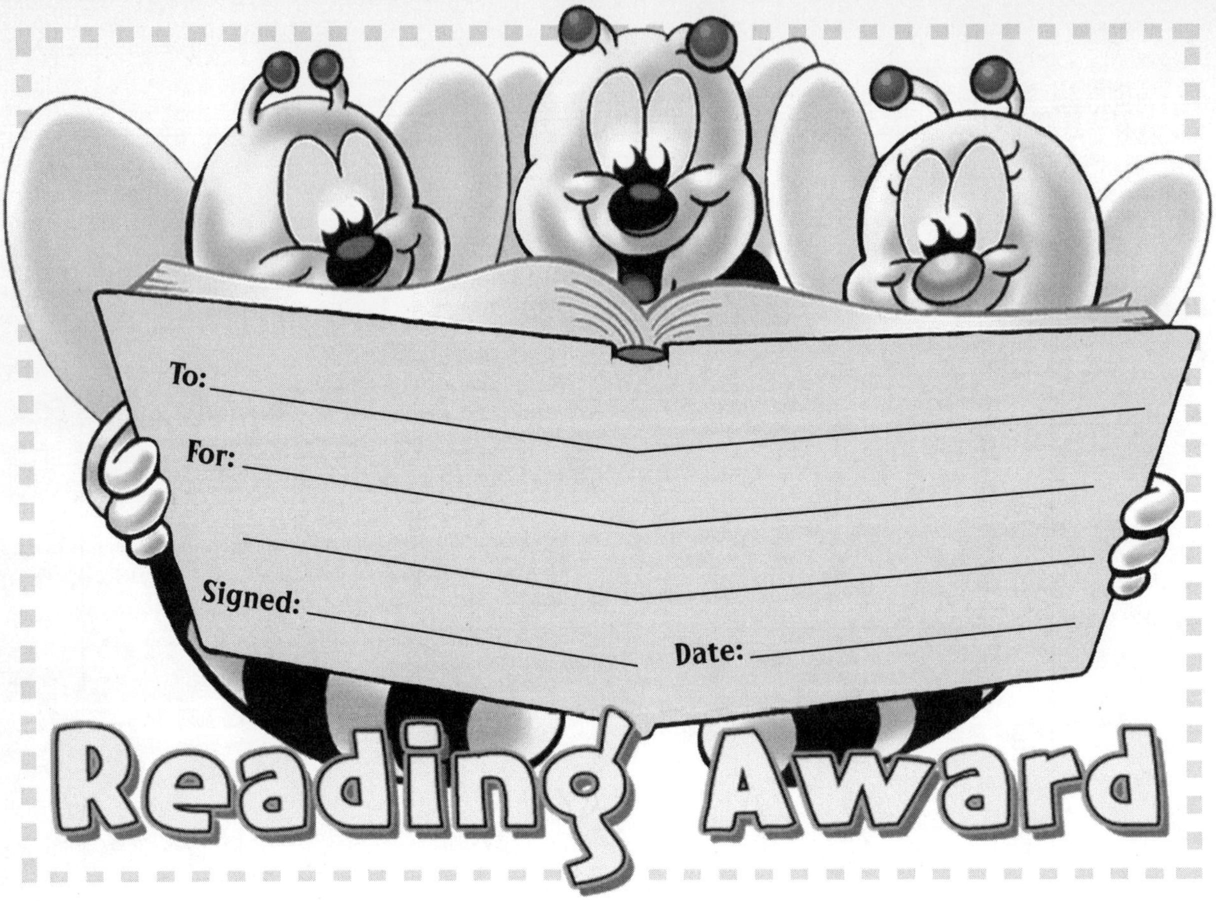
To:
For:
Signed:
Date:
Reading Award

To:
For:
Signed:
Date:
Reading Award

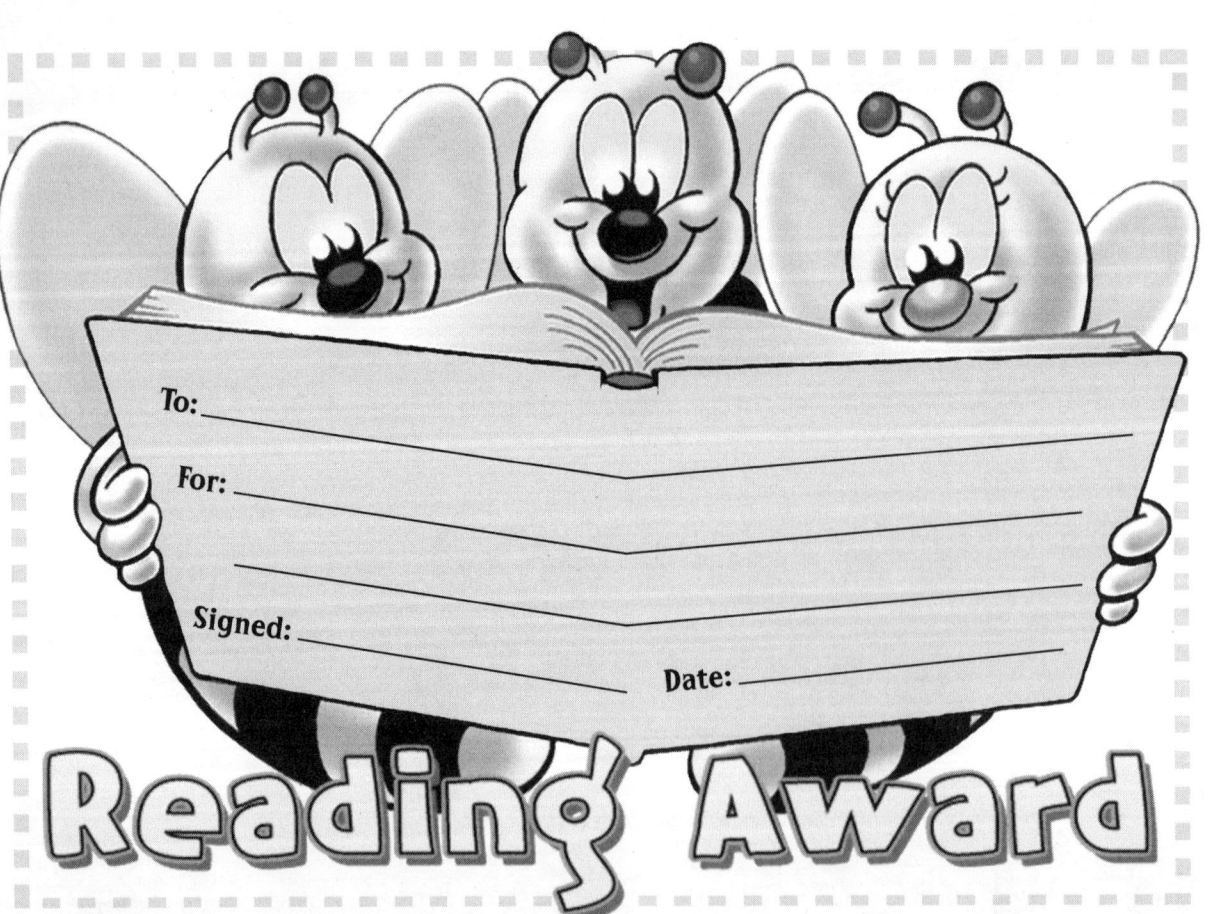

Gold Medals and Blue Ribbons

Praise students for good reading. Reproduce, color, cut out and keep on hand for generous praise. Add your own messages to the center of each.

Hip, Hip, Hooray!

_____
is rolling towards success in reading.

Signed:_____

Hip, Hip, Hooray!

_____
is rolling towards success in reading.

Signed:_____